Catfish Fingerlings Production:

How To Successfully Hatch Fries

AGRICFY FARMS LIMITED

 https://agricfy.com **+2348166416803**

 www.youtube.com/@AgricfyFarms

responsibility or blame be held against the publisher for any reparation, damages, or monetary loss due to the information herein, either directly or indirectly.

Respective authors own all copyrights not held by the publisher. The information herein is solely offered for informational purposes and is universal. The presentation of the information is without a contract or any type of guarantee assurance.

The trademarks used are without any consent, and the trademark publication is without permission or backing by the trademark owner. All trademarks and brands within this book are for clarifying purposes only and owned by the owners, not affiliated with this document.

4

Contents

Introduction To Fish Farming

Fish farming also known as fish culture, is a type of animal husbandry that involves raising finfish in controlled environments.

This practice is part of a larger field called aquaculture, which is akin to agriculture but in water.

In aquaculture, finfish and shellfish are nurtured to reach a size suitable for the market.

Benefits of Fish Farming

Fish farming offers several key benefits:

- **Consistent Fish Supply**: You can count on a constant and reliable source of fish.

- **Convenience and Reliability**: It's a dependable way to produce fish.

- **Safety**: Fish farming carries fewer risks than other animal.

- **Minimal Hassle:** It creates less inconvenience and is virtually odorless.

- **Quiet Operation**: Unlike poultry farming, it doesn't generate noise disturbances.

- **No Need for Clearing Land:** Unlike poultry and cattle farming, fish farming doesn't require extensive land clearing.

- **High-Profit Potential**: Fish farming can be highly profitable.

Fish farming is a practical and efficient way to make money from animal farming while minimizing many of the challenges associated with other forms of animal farming.

Types of Fish Farming

Fish farming is a broad term that covers a lot of different methods and species of fish, all of which are tailored to different environments and goals.

Catfish farming is one of the most profitable types of fish farming due to its high consumption ratio.

Other types of fish farming include tilapia, trout, salmon, and carp farming, each with unique requirements and considerations.

However, our focus here is on catfish farming. As we dive into this topic, we'll explore different aspects of catfish farming, such as catfish hatching and equipment for catfish farming, among others.

Catfish Hatching

Catfish hatching is the process of incubating fertilized catfish eggs in controlled conditions to allow them to develop into newly hatched fry, commonly referred to as fries.

In simpler words, it is when you take catfish eggs and keep them in a warm and safe environment so they can grow into baby fish called fingerlings.

It is an artificial fertilization process because it involves manual intervention in the reproduction process, including hormone injection and controlled breeding environments, to ensure successful fertilization and hatching.

Overall, hatching catfish is one of the most fundamental and profitable aspects of catfish farming. Sure, it's one of the most challenging aspects of catfish farming, but the benefits you'll enjoy will be worth it if you can overcome these challenges.

Let's explore some essential details about catfish hatching.

Catfish Reproduction: Natural Vs. Artificial Breeding Cycles

Catfish in their natural habitat reach sexual maturity after 2-3 years and breed during the rainy season. After spawning (reproduction), their gonads (reproductive organs) gradually shrink, and they don't breed again until the next rainy season.

However, in an artificial environment (ponds), catfish can reach sexual maturity in 7-10 months and weigh between 200 and 500 grams.

Furthermore, fish usually don't spawn in their natural habitat if the water level doesn't rise and flood the surrounding areas. This is because the rise in water level signals the fish that it's time to reproduce.

However, when raising a fish in an artificial habitat (fish pond), you can get the fish to spawn (reproduce) by giving them artificial hormones from the pituitary gland.

Fish raised in ponds usually stay fertile for several months out of the year, which matches up with their natural breeding cycle. A brood (mature/adult) fish can be bred multiple times in these months.

Overall, catfish raised from egg to maturity in a hatchery remain mature during the whole year, and regression of the gonads does not occur. It means you can get larvae/juveniles (baby fish) all year round and keep reproducing adult fish commercially. This is why catfish hatching is profitable.

How To Prepare And Assess Broodstock (Adult) Fish For Hatching

To ensure the successful hatching of catfish eggs, it's crucial to prepare and assess the adult male and female fish properly. Here are step-by-step instructions to help you through this process:

Step 1: Collecting Adult Fish

- Begin by carefully selecting adult male and female fish from your fish pond. These fish will serve as the parents of the next generation of catfish.

Step 2: Disinfection

- Before bringing the selected adult fish into the incubator, disinfecting them is highly recommended. It helps prevent the transfer of harmful bacteria to the eggs and newly hatched larvae, ensuring a healthier start for the young fish. (It is advisable to disinfect the fish with a 50–150 p.p.m. formalin bath for three hours before you bring them into the incubator).

Step 3: Assessing Female Maturity

Determining the maturity of female catfish is essential for successful breeding. You can assess their maturity using the following method:

- Gently cover the fish's head with a towel to keep it calm and still.

- Carefully turn the fish onto its back.

- Using your finger or thumb, apply light pressure on the abdomen, moving from the head towards the tail.

- If the female is mature, you will notice the release of greenish eggs.

Step 4: More Reliable Assessment

For a more accurate assessment of female maturity, you can follow this method:

- Gently insert a cannula with a suitable diameter into the papilla located inside the ovary.

- Place the other end of the cannula into your mouth and carefully create a gentle suction.

- Withdraw the cannula, and you will observe the release of approximately thirty eggs onto a glass slide.

- These steps ensure that you have healthy, mature fish ready for breeding, laying the foundation for successful catfish hatching.

- In conclusion, careful selection, disinfection, and accurate assessment of the maturity of adult catfish are essential steps in preparing them for hatching. This meticulous process sets the stage for a successful breeding program, producing robust catfish fingerlings.

Materials Needed In Fish Hatchery

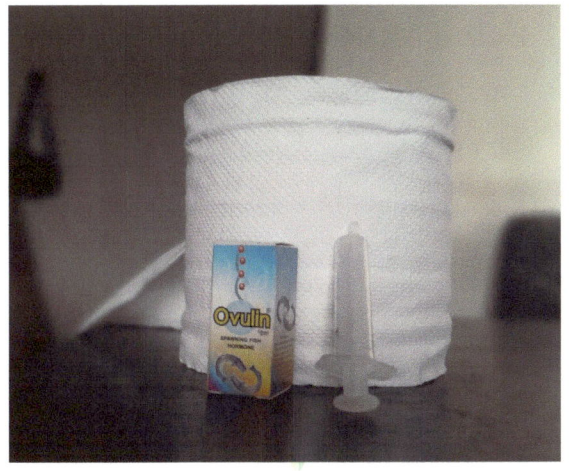

- A table of about 50 x 100 cm
- Net
- Scale
- Ruler
- Trays
- Towel/Clean piece of cloth
- Canula (outer diameter 2-2 1/2 mm; inner diameter 1.2-1-5 mm)
- Syringes (1ml) and needles
- Sharp knife, wire cutter

- Mortar
- A pair of scissors, a pair of sharp-pointed tweezers
- Bottle of physiological salt, solution 0.9%
- Water analysis kit
- Thermometers
- Glassware
- Brushes

More Hatchery Equipment and their Uses

Incubator – This is the place where you will be hatching the catfish's eggs.

Water pH Tester Kit – The first thing you need to do before deciding where the hatchery process will take place is to test the water's pH. This is important because you don't want the acidity and alkalinity of the water to be too much or insufficient.

If this happens, the fish will not survive the hatching process. The recommended pH level of your water should be between **6.5** and **7.5**.

Broodstock – These are the fish you will be using for the process. They are adult female and male catfish used to hatch eggs. The desired size of the fish for the best results is 1kg.

Scale – This is an instrument that will be used to measure the size of the fish. You can use either a digital or manual scale of different sizes.

Synthetic Hormone – This is used for induced breeding. You will inject the female catfish with this substance and leave it for at least 8 hours for the eggs to come together and get ready for insemination. The commonly used synthetic hormones are Ovaprim, Ovatide, and Ovulin.

Syringe – This will be used to draw the synthetic hormone and inject it into the female catfish.

Saline Solution – This is used during the hatchery process to mix the eggs with the milt (sperm).

Some people use salt solutions, while others use seawater. If you don't know the right quantity of salt to mix with water, just go with seawater or freshwater.

Better still, you can use saline water that is mostly used in hospitals (drip).

Spawning Net – This is the net you will spread on the prepared water. The spawning net will hold the eggs, and the hatched eggs will fall into the water while the rotten eggs will remain on the net till you remove the net from the water.

Water Analysis Kit/Thermometer - A water analysis kit analyzes water parameters. This kit can include a pH meter and thermometer. As you may already know, the pH meter measures the pH level of the water you'll be using for hatching, while a thermometer measures the temperature of the hatching house or room.

Bowl – You'll use this to strip the eggs and mix them with the milt.

Towel – To hold the female catfish during stripping so the fish doesn't fall off.

Some other items on the list above might not be necessary for you to have, but it is good you know them.

Let me also say that you cannot have everything on your farm; just try to have the major ones and make do with them.

Managing Your Hatchery Equipment

When it comes to managing hatchery equipment, here are some things to keep in mind.

Containers: You'll need containers to house your broodfish temporarily. These can be made from wood barrels, concrete, or wooden tanks. I recommend using PVC barrels over iron ones.

Stack seven containers on one side of the hatchery, ensuring they're on wooden beams or platforms 5-10cm off the ground.

Container Setup: Each container should have a way to get water in (called water inlet), a way to get water out (water outlet), and a way to let water out if it gets too full (overflow). You can make it easier to drain the water by attaching a plastic tube to the outlet. This tube can also help you control the water level in the container. To get the water level right, loop the tube around a hook at the desired height. With a bit of practice, you'll be able to get the water level perfect every time.

Safety Measures: Ensure the container's lid is locked down tight with a sturdy wire fence. Catfish are known for their jumping skills, so placing some heavy stones on the screen is essential to keep them from jumping out.

Individual Housing: You'll need about 4-5 female and 2 male fish for a typical artificially induced breeding cycle.

Incubator: An incubation gutter is required to fertilize the eggs. The incubation gutter should have the following dimensions: 200 x 50 x 30cm. It can be made from wood, polyester, or concrete. Iron and copper should not be used, as they are often poisonous to fish.

Screens/Frames. A screen should be placed before the overflow (at the top of the container) to prevent juveniles (the baby fish) escaping. The screen can be made of two wooden frames that exactly fit in the gutter. In between the frames, a net/mesh cloth measuring 0.5 - 0.7 mm should be properly fixed between both frames.

How To Hatch Catfish Fries: The Hatching Process

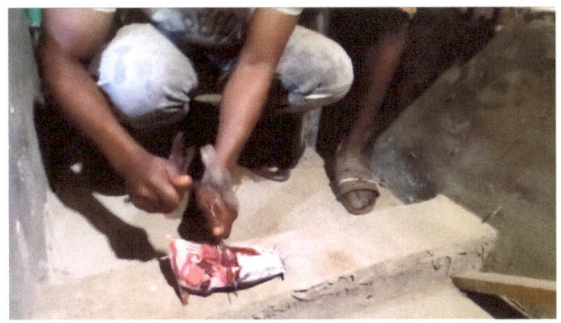

1. Collecting Pituitaries for Catfish Breeding

To collect pituitaries for catfish breeding, follow these simple steps:

- Choose two donors, ideally one male and one female, both weighing around 500g each. The male's testes can be used, too. Ensure the male donors are killed and decapitated no sooner than one hour before injecting the female spawner.

- Turn the donor's head upside down and remove the lower jaw. The pituitary gland is located inside the skull.

- Open the palate of the mouth using a pair of pincers at the indicated point. The pituitary is a small, pinkish-white, roundish organ located on the brain's underside.

- Collect the pituitary in a solution of physiological salt. Prepare the solution by dissolving 9 grams of common table salt in 1 litre of filtered water.

- Grind the pituitaries immediately in a mortar and draw the resulting pituitary suspension into a syringe.

- Inject the suspension of freshly collected pituitaries as soon as possible for optimal results.

If you need to store freshly collected pituitaries for up to a month, follow this procedure:

- Place the pituitaries in a vial filled with acetone (1 ml per pituitary) immediately after extraction.

- Refresh the acetone after ten minutes.

- Renew the acetone again after 8 hours.

- Drain the acetone entirely after 24 hours.

- Dry the pituitaries in the shade by allowing them to evaporate.

- Store the dry, yellow-brown pituitaries in a sealed vial in a cool place.

2. Injecting the Female Spawner

To inject the suspended pituitaries effectively, follow these simple steps:

- Prepare your tools: Attach a 2.5 - 3.0 cm needle with a 0.6 - 0.7 mm diameter to your syringe. Make sure there's no air in the syringe.

- Prepare the Female Spawner: Cover the head of the female spawner (typically around 500g in weight) with a towel.

- Insert the Needle: Insert the needle at a 30 - 34° angle into the dorsal muscles, about 2 - 2.5 cm deep in the direction of the tail.

- Inject Slowly: Inject the suspension into the muscles while gently retracting the syringe a few millimeters.

- Massage the Injection Area: After the injection, lightly massage the area to distribute the suspension evenly throughout the muscles.

- Wait for Ovulation: Return the fish to its container and wait for approximately 12 hours. During this time, the female's belly will noticeably swell due to the water absorption in the ovary as the eggs mature and ovulate.

These steps will help you perform the injection process effectively and ensure the best results for catfish fingerling production.

Identifying And Selecting Genders For Successful Catfish Breeding

Identification of the Male and Female Fish

To distinguish between male and female catfish, look for these key traits.

- Female catfish, especially those carrying eggs, have a larger stomach area, while males have a smaller one.
- Additionally, males have longer sex organs, while females have round ones.
- When selecting females for hatchery purposes, consider those weighing at least 1 kg with ample eggs.
- It's ideal to choose females that are around 1 year old, as indicated by eggs that range in color from dark golden green to golden.
- For males, check that their sex organ, found just below the anus, is longer than the upper part of the anal fin.

These distinctions will help you make informed choices for your catfish breeding program.

Guidelines For Choosing The Right Fish For Your Hatchery

When selecting fish for your hatchery, you have a few options:

1. Use Fish from Your Pond: If you already have fish in your pond, you can consider using them for breeding.

2. Buy from Other Fish Farmers: Alternatively, you can purchase fish from fellow fish farmers.

Important Note: If you buy fish from the wild, it's best to do so only during the rainy season.

However, one crucial rule to remember is

3. Avoid Cross-Breeds (Hybrids): Never use cross-breeds like Heteroclarias as your brood

stock for hatchery purposes.

Heteroclarias is a hybrid resulting from the cross-breeding of Heterobranchus and Clarias. Because it's a hybrid, it's not suitable for hatchery purposes.

Following these guidelines ensures that you're working with the right fish stock for successful catfish fingerling production.

Male And Female Diagram

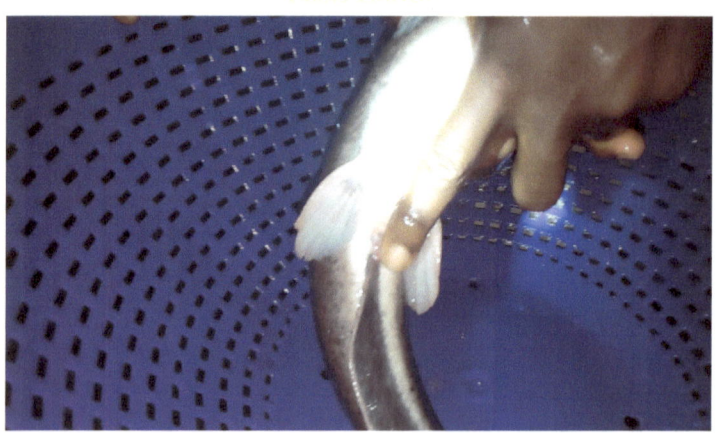

Taking Care of The Fish

Keep the catfish meant for hatching purposes separate in different plastic containers filled with good (well or borehole) water and covered with an aerated lid supported with a heavy object like a stone.

Extraction of Milt, Stripping, And Fertilization

Requirements

1. Sharp knife

2. Mature male catfish and the injected female catfish

3. Handkerchief

4. Tissue (toilet) roll

5. Semi-deep plastic bowl

6. Clean water (borehole or well water)

7. Plastic cup

8. Torchlight

The Process

Step 1:

To determine if it's time for stripping, begin by inspecting the fish. To check if a female fish is ready, look for a swollen stomach. If you see it, she's good to go. For added certainty, gently press the stomach while holding the fish. If you notice that the eggs are naturally emerging, it's a confirmation. Return the fish to the latency tank.

Step 2:

Prepare the male fish chosen for hatchery use. Begin by removing its head and making a vertical cut along the belly using a sharp knife to expose the stomach area. Inside, you'll find the milt, which contains sperm. Carefully detach and clean it, using a toilet roll to remove any blood or stains. Finally, wrap it in clean tissue paper for further use.

Step 3:

Remove the fish from the latency container. gently massage it to release her eggs onto a small plastic plate.

Step 4:

Use a sharp new razor blade to cut the mint in a vertical line. Let the milky liquid drip gently onto the eggs. Next, rinse them by carefully adding small drops of saline solution to cover the milt and letting it flow over the eggs. Do this while gently spreading the solution across the eggs on the plastic plate.

Step 5:

Gently pour a saline solution over the eggs while stirring for about 80 seconds. Stop when the eggs are evenly distributed on the plate.

Step 6:

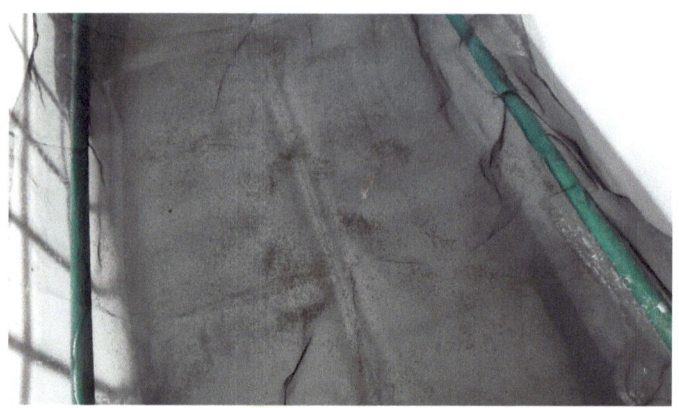

Finally, gently spread the eggs over the incubator's spawning mop evenly.

After spreading the eggs, cover the hatchery pond for over 24 hours to enable the eggs to hatch.

The number of hours might be more depending on the weather conditions in which you hatch.

Pond Management

Preparing the Hatchery for Fry to Fingerling Stage

To transition your fries into fingerlings successfully, precise water management in the hatchery is crucial. Here's a straightforward guide:

Water Inlet Setup: Start by introducing water into the incubator using a small hose or tap, ensuring a gentle flow of one litre per minute.

Simultaneously, adjust the water outlet to match this flow rate. Place the water inlet hose or tap on one side of the incubator, opposite the outlet pipe.

Safeguarding the Environment: To protect your fingerlings, cover most of the incubator with tarpaulin or wooden boards. Leave the area around the water inlet hose uncovered, but protect it with a mosquito net. This not only keeps out potential predators but also maintains an optimal environment for hatching and nurturing the fries.

Handling Catfish Fingerling Hatchery: Once the incubation and hatching process is finished (usually around 24 hours after spraying), wait for up to six hours (after the initial 24 hours) for most, if not all, of the eggs to hatch, especially in hot weather or during the dry season.

After this period, remove the mop and increase the water flow into the incubation pond to clean up any potential pollution caused by unhatched eggs, which are whitish.

To prevent water pollution, carefully siphon out the unhatched eggs. Use a small (1 mm) water hose, point it at the suspended or settled unhatched eggs, and let the water's force suck them up and flush them through the hose into the pond.

Next, regularly check the pond water to ensure it remains clean and clear. Make sure the water inflow and outflow systems are working effectively.

Additionally, wait to feed the newly hatched fries until 48 hours after the hatchery process is complete.

Nursery Gutters

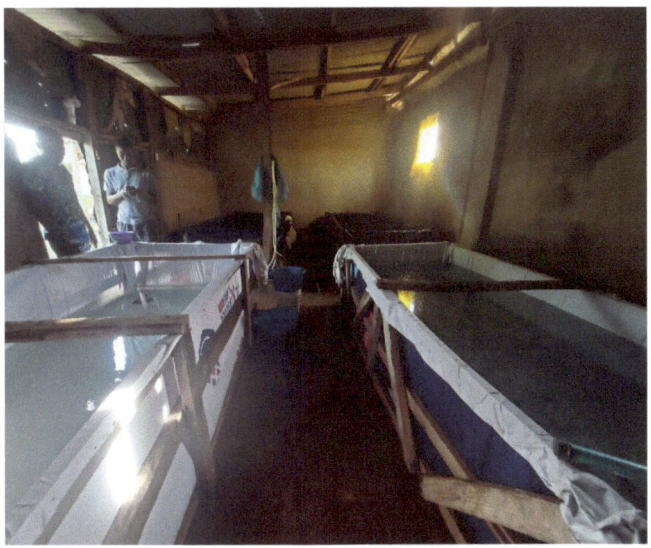

During the initial two weeks of nursing catfish fry, you can follow the same conditions as you did in the incubation gutter.

However, once the fry population grows significantly

after the second week, dividing them into four nursery gutters is best.

This division ensures enough water volume for their growth and maintains good water quality, especially when feeding them more.

Each nursery gutter should have a 60W lamp above the outlet and an automatic feeder on the cover above it to ensure proper care for the fry.

The Fry

In three days after hatching, the yolk sac is completely absorbed. During this time, the young fish's weight increases to around 3.0 mg as they absorb water.

In the initial two weeks, the number of young fish, or fries, decreases from 65,000 to 60,000. Then, in the following three weeks (the third, fourth, and fifth), it drops from 60,000 to 48,000 due to natural mortality.

We can visualize the growth in the average weight of the fry throughout the entire rearing period.

Feeding

In the initial two weeks, feed the fry four times a day until they're full. You can use live zooplankton or Artemia naupliar for their meals.

Zooplankton Feeding

To provide top-notch nutrition for catfish fingerlings, it's crucial to collect fresh zooplankton such as rotifers, cladocerans, and copepods daily.

You can source from natural environments or specially prepared ponds to boost plankton growth. However, when using pond water, be mindful, as it can potentially introduce fish diseases into the nursery.

Artemia Feeding

Artemia feeding refers to the process of providing Artemia nauplii (baby brine shrimp) as a nutritional source to young fish, mainly fry. These tiny Artemia nauplii are a valuable and highly nutritious food for many species of fish during their early stages of development. As such, it is a crucial process for hatching catfish.

You can easily find canned Artemia cysts in many tropical countries nowadays. To hatch them into baby brine shrimp, place the cysts in aerated water at a temperature of 28-30°C. You can use either sea salt (35g per litre) or common table salt.

Ensure oxygen levels stay above three parts per million (ppm). Within 24-36 hours, the cysts will hatch, and you can separate the baby Artemia, called nauplii, from the empty shells.

You can feed the nauplii to the fry while they are still alive or frozen. During feeding, pause the water flow in the gutter for 10-15 minutes for best results.

Foreign Feeds

This feeding method is common if you're in an area where it is difficult to get Zooplankton and Artemia.

As a beginner in the hatching section, you can buy foreign feeds from different outlets and give your fries when they begin eating.

Depending on your location, you'll find the brands I use and recommend for you to give your fries.

1. Coppens - 0.2mm
2. Skretting - Gamma Wean (This is way more expensive than any feed you could buy in the market)

Fries and Fingerlings Handling

In fish farming, just like in crop farming, the key to success lies in the quality of the seeds we use. In this case, these seeds are fry and fingerlings. To ensure a bountiful harvest, preserving and protecting these seeds from diseases and other threats is crucial.

To achieve this, it's essential to provide the right equipment and conditions for the healthy growth of our fry and fingerlings. This step is vital in obtaining robust seeds for successful fish farming. Some of the equipment needed include;

- Plastic bags of different sizes
- Gas regulators
- Oxygen cylinder,
- Strong twine for tapping the bags
- Scoop nets of fine mesh,
- Plastic buckets.

Handle them gently in oxygen-rich containers to ensure fish survival during pond transfers. Additionally, let the fish adapt slowly before introducing them to new ponds.

It helps maintain a high survival rate.

Guidelines For Transporting And Stocking Fish

- Use a plastic basin (keg, polybag, or metal bucket for a short distance).

- Use a small net with a handle to scoop out small fish

- Transfer the fish with a scoop net into the container gently.

- Compare the pond temperature with the bucket water temperature. Slowly add the pond water to the bucket until it reaches the same temperature.

- Place the bucket slowly into the pond so the fry swims out themselves.

- Check the condition of the pond walls. Repair weak points and leaks.

- Walk around the pond and check the fence for holes. Do repairs immediately. Remove frogs, toads, and tadpoles and their eggs.

- Remove submerged water weeds. The plants reduce light penetration in the water; they compete with plankton for nutrients and may cause difficulty collecting fingerlings during harvesting.

By following these steps, you should have no issues with the transporting and stocking process.

Fingerling Harvesting Process

Harvesting fingerlings is a crucial step in catfish production. To do it effectively, follow these steps:

- Timing is Key: Begin draining the pond a few hours before sunrise when it's still cool. Let the water level decrease gradually.

- Prevent Escape: Place a fine mesh screen in front of the outlet pipe to keep the fingerlings from escaping. Connect a screened box to the outlet as the water level nears the pond bottom.

- Collect in the Box: As you remove the lowest shelf in the monk and the fine mesh, fingerlings will gather in the harvest box.

- Size and Weight: Harvested fingerlings typically measure 3-6 cm and weigh 1-3g each. Survival rates can vary from 0% to 30%, yielding around 20,000 fingerlings.

- Avoid Cannibalism: During the nursing period, some fingerlings may grow faster than others, leading to potential cannibalism. Separate the larger ones from the rest before transferring them to fattening ponds to prevent losses.

Separation Method: To separate fingerlings by size:

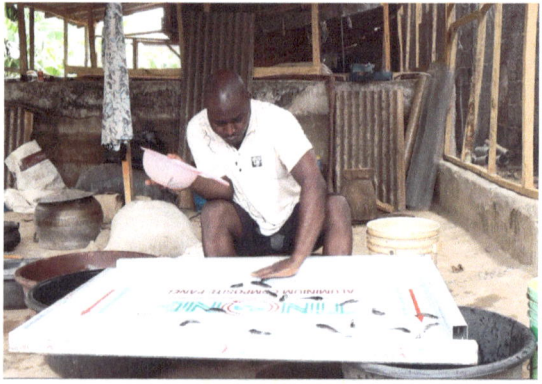

- Place the fish on a smooth table with frames and holes.
- Use a specific hole for each size class.
- Position containers with water under the holes.

By following these steps, you can streamline the harvesting process and ensure the healthy growth of your catfish fingerlings.

Stocking Considerations:

- Don't overcrowd the pond; avoid putting more than 500 fingerlings of 2g/3g size. Ensure they have enough space to access the water's surface to breathe.
- Keep the fish away from direct sunlight during the harvesting process.
- After harvesting, quickly introduce fingerlings into the fattening ponds. It's essential to use fingerlings of similar sizes for stocking.

Nursery Pond Maintenance Guidelines

To ensure your nursery pond remains productive, it's essential to perform after-care. So, before starting a new production cycle, take the following steps:

- Assess and Remove Excess Silt: While using the pond, dirt can build up at the bottom, mostly from clay that's suspended in the water that comes in.

A little bit of silt can be good for your pond. It can help plants grow and provide food for fish. But too much silt can be a problem.

It can block sunlight, suffocate plants, and make it hard for fish to breathe.

So, if you see a lot of silt in your pond, it's a good idea to clean it up.

- Disinfect the Pond Bottom: Apply quicklime at 10-15 kg per area to disinfect the damp pond bottom. Allow the pond to dry for several days until the clay surface cracks.

- Prepare the Pond: Once the pond is dry and the clay has cracked, follow the preparation steps below;

    → Wash the ponds with salt and rinse with clean water
    → Use a soft brush or foam to clean
    → Rinse the pond again with water
    → Fill the pond with water to your desired

point

Maintaining your nursery pond in this way ensures optimal conditions for successful catfish fingerling production.

Catfish Fries Diseases

In water, diseases can quickly spread among catfish through their gills and skin. When raised under ideal conditions, African catfish can typically withstand common waterborne threats like viruses, bacteria, and parasites.

However, poor water quality, improper feeding, rough fish handling, and a stressful environment can weaken their resistance.

This can lead to a weakened immune system, making catfish more susceptible to sudden disease outbreaks, which are especially risky for fry and fingerlings since they haven't yet developed strong immunity.

Stressed or diseased catfish often display abnormal behavior, such as reduced appetite, nervous or erratic swimming patterns, staying near the water's surface in a vertical position, or showing clinical symptoms like damaged barbels or fins, white or red-brown skin spots, and pop-eye, among others.

Remember that these symptoms aren't unique to a specific disease, so a precise diagnosis requires the laboratory techniques described below.

Daily monitoring of ponds is crucial, especially during feeding times when catfish tend to gather at the water's surface.

If any doubt arises, collecting fish for a closer examination is advisable. For diagnosing bacterial, fungal, and parasitic diseases, you'll need to create and analyze squash preparations from the skin, gill filaments, intestines, etc. A microscope with magnification ranging from "x 40 to x 1000" is essential for identifying diseases. Once you identify a disease, specific treatment can often begin promptly.

Bacterial Diseases

Symptoms: Diseased catfish may stay vertically near the water's surface or exhibit unusual swimming behavior.

White spots, particularly around the mouth and fins, can be observed on their skin.

To diagnose, take a smear of gills and skin and examine it under a microscope; you'll likely find elongated motile rods.

Diagnosis: Myxobacteria

Conclusion

Hatching catfish is a fascinating endeavor that can be affordable, especially if you're not going for commercial purposes.

Hatching catfish fingerlings is surprisingly straightforward, typically taking about 24 to 36 hours, making it accessible to anyone. However, the real challenge begins once you've successfully hatched your fish.

During the first two weeks following the hatchery process, the survival of your fish hinges on your careful attention.

You must handle the fry with utmost care when:

- Changing the water,

- Feeding,

- Siphoning the pond, and

- You need to sort them.

This part of the process must be taken seriously and demands special care and attention.

Not many people are lucky with hatching catfish and fries production but with this guide, I can assure you to fire on with your production.

This is not to say that you won't encounter any challenges in the process, you will but you can easily overcome them.

FOLLOW ON ALL SOCIALS

https://www.facebook.com/Agricfy/

https://www.instagram.com/agricfy/

https://www.pinterest.com/Agricfy/

https://agricfy.com

www.youtube.com/@AgricfyFarms